Arm Yourself Against the Enemy's Scheme

A Taste of When Godly People Do Ungodly Things

Beth Moore

Published by LifeWay Press®
© 2008 Beth Moore

No part of this book may be reproduced or transmitted
in any form or by any means, electronic or mechanical,
including photocopying and recording, or by any information
storage or retrieval system, except as may be expressly
permitted in writing by the publisher. Requests for permission
should be addressed in writing to LifeWay Press®;
One LifeWay Plaza; Nashville, TN 37234-0175.

ISBN 978-1-4158-6530-9
Item 005139184

Dewey decimal classification: 235.4
Subject heading: SPIRITUAL WARFARE \
TEMPTATION \ CHRISTIAN LIFE

Unless otherwise indicated, Scripture quotations are from
the Holy Bible, New International Version, copyright ©
1973, 1978, 1984 by International Bible Society. Scripture
quotations identified KJV are from the King James Version.
Scripture quotations marked HCSB® are taken from the Holman
Christian Standard Bible®, copyright © 1999, 2000, 2002, 2003
by Holman Bible Publishers. Used by permission.

To order additional copies of this resource, write to LifeWay
Church Resources Customer Service; One LifeWay Plaza;
Nashville, TN 37234-0013; e-mail *orderentry@lifeway.com*;
fax (615) 251-5933; phone toll free (800) 458-2772; order online at
www.lifeway.com; or visit the LifeWay Christian Store serving you.

Printed in the United States of America

Leadership and Adult Publishing
LifeWay Church Resources
One LifeWay Plaza
Nashville, TN 37234-0175

CONTENTS

INTRODUCTION

A strange thing began to happen soon after my books *Breaking Free* and *Praying God's Word* were released. Probably because I admit to such a flawed and sinful past, letters began stacking on my desk from Christians confessing, often for the very first time, to harrowing rounds of defeat at the hands of the Devil.

Satan has attacked man since his creation, but I'd like to suggest that something about this spiritual phenomenon might have taken demonic assault to a whole new level. In the course of my ministry I've read countless letters, and I have come to discern the difference between blatant accounts of mercifully forgiven rebellion and the testimonials I'm talking about. Beloved, I believe Satan is more active today in attacking Christians than ever before.

Three streams of evidence lead me to my conclusions. As we proceed, consider the significance of each.

1. A Growing Stack of Testimonies

What has terrified me is my growing pile of letters from believers who loved God and walked with Him faithfully for years and then found themselves suddenly overtaken by a tidal wave of temptation and unholy assault. Many Christians are convinced such things can't happen. "Not to good Christians." They are wrong.

I believe many accounts of formerly pure lives suddenly knee-deep in the mire are absolutely authentic. Not one presents him- or herself as an innocent victim. They are horrified and taken aback at what they have done and at what they appear capable of doing. I've repeatedly heard renditions of the statement, "For the life of me, I can't figure out how something like this could have happened."

2. Scripture Supports the Idea

I don't care how many testimonials I receive, I would not give their suggestions that godly people can do ungodly things a second thought except that Scripture supports the idea: "I am fearful, lest that even as the serpent beguiled Eve by his cunning, so your minds may be corrupted and seduced from wholehearted and sincere and pure devotion to Christ" (2 Cor. 11:3, AMP).

Those who are wholehearted and sincere in devotion to Christ can be beguiled by the enemy, whose utmost fantasy is to corrupt and seduce. Not only are the godly capable of suddenly sprawling into a ditch from a solid, upright path, but many do. As the days blow off the kingdom calendar, I am convinced that the casualty numbers are growing. To say that the body of Christ would be shocked to know how bloody and bruised by defeat we are is an understatement. God, however, is most assuredly not shocked. You see, He told us this was coming.

3. The End of the Age

In Christ's discourse to His disciples concerning the signs of His coming and the end of the age, He emphatically warned of an increase in deception, lawlessness, and wickedness. In Matthew 24 Jesus told of a time of severe persecution, a time of "great distress, unequaled from the beginning of the world until now" (MATT. 24:21). These warnings have applied to all ages, but many Bible scholars believe they point specifically to the war going on today.

While fresh winds of the Spirit are blowing in many of our churches and a double portion of the anointing is bestowed on many believers, the Word strongly suggests that we are occupying earth during the scariest time in human history. You need only look as far as your own community to be able to stare 2 Timothy 3:1-5 in the face:

"There will be terrible times in the last days. People will be lovers of themselves, lovers of

money, boastful, proud, abusive, disobedient to their parents, ungrateful, unholy, without love, unforgiving, slanderous, without self-control, brutal, not lovers of the good, treacherous, rash, conceited, lovers of pleasure rather than lovers of God—having a form of godliness but denying its power."

I believe in these last days Satan has two primary motivations: (1) to exact revenge on God by wreaking havoc on His children and (2) to try to incapacitate the believer's God-given ability to overcome him.

Revelation 12:11 says, "They overcame [the Devil] by the blood of the Lamb and by the word of their testimony." Those of us who have received Christ as personal Savior are the Holy Spirit's dwelling places (1 COR. 6:19-20). We are covered by Jesus' precious blood, and neither Satan nor his demons can come near us.

Satan's worst nightmare is being overcome—especially by measly mortals. He knows the Bible says we overcome our accuser in two primary ways. If he can do nothing about the blood of the Lamb covering the redeemed, what's a Devil to do? Go for the word of their testimony! Satan is out to destroy the testimony of every believer in Christ. His murderous eye is on the sparrow, and he doesn't have much time.

Many people who by the grace of God have never been had by the Devil wrongly assume that all departures from godliness are nothing but defiance, rebellion, and proofs of inauthenticity. They have no idea of the suffering involved when someone with a genuine heart for God slips from the path.

Tangling with the Devil, whom the Bible calls a "roaring lion" who is trying his hardest to devour believers, can constitute authentic suffering (SEE 1 PET. 5:8). In fact, I have suffered more at the flesh-ripping paws of the raging lion than anything else.

Now that countless letters, frantic phone calls, and face-to-face testimonies have found their way to my office, I realize I am far from the only true lover of God whom Satan has tried to destroy. Although I don't character- ize myself as godly, I will tell you that I loved God more than anything else at the times of my greatest demonic assault.

I know plenty of others whom I would not hesitate to call godly, yet they suddenly found themselves objects of overwhelming battles against godliness. Based on the find- ings landing on my desk, increasing numbers of dear brothers and sisters throughout the world are undergoing tremendous suffering at the Devil's paws.

Beloved, Satan hates to let go of a captive. He also hates being exposed as the fraud that he is. My specific prayer for the message of this booklet is threefold:

- that God will use these pages to shed light on Satan's campaign to seduce the saints
- that God will use this message to remind battered believers how loved

they are and how much the Father
longs for their restoration

- that many readers will wise up and
fortify their lives before Satan traps
them into something ungodly

Seductions can vary in type, but one thing is for sure: They are tailor-made to catch the believer off guard. Dear body of Christ, it's time we put down the popguns of yester-year's church. Satan is waging a worldwide nuclear war.

Chapter 1
UNDERSTAND SATAN'S PLOT

Many believers have a wrong conception of Satan's power. They think he is somehow parallel to or as powerful as God. Satan is far more powerful, personal, and conniving than many believe. Let's be very careful, however, not to dream of giving Satan more credit than he is due. While he is tremendously potent, armed, and dangerous, he is not the equal of the Most High God.

The Lord maintains authority over all powers and principalities. Satan is merely a created being, but that doesn't mean he is not a threat. At our strongest moments we are no match for him. Only Almighty God can overpower Satan. We walk in the victory Christ won for us only when we are "strong in the Lord and in his mighty power" (Eph. 6:10).

Christ Himself referred to Satan as the prince of this world system in John 12:31 and 16:11. He also portrayed Satan as already defeated (LUKE 10:18). So why is a defeated enemy so hard at work in a post-Calvary world? This illustration helps.

In the United States our presidential elections occur in November, but the new president does not assume the position until January. Let's see if I can explain the parallel. I believe in a literal reign of Christ on this earth. I am convinced Scripture teaches that Christ Jesus will visibly return to earth and rule in righteousness for a thousand years. I also believe that the "scroll" described in Revelation 5 is somewhat of a title deed to the world system. God permitted that authority to fall into Satan's hands for a time, after man's forced exodus from the garden. One day soon God will place that title deed back in the hands of its rightful ruler. At the God-ordained time, Christ will return to earth, conquer every foe, and take His seat of authority.

We now live in the period leading up to Christ taking His rightful throne. Today Christ is Lord of lords and King of kings, but His kingdom is currently not of this world (SEE JOHN 18:36). The day is coming when the nature of the kingdom will change. The Christ who reigns today in believers will reign outwardly and absolutely. He will take back what the enemy has stolen.

As if Satan needed any more reason to rage, his situation becomes even bleaker. Peter described the consummation of the age in these words:

> *"The heavens will disappear with a roar; the elements will be destroyed by fire, and the earth and everything in it will be laid bare. … That day will bring about the destruction of the heavens by fire, and the elements will melt in the*

*heat. But in keeping with his promise
we are looking forward to a new heaven
and a new earth, the home of righteousness"* (2 PET. 3:10,12-13).

Don't miss the significance of Peter's
words from Satan's perspective. All
beings will be in their eternal state from
this time forward—whether redeemed in
the presence of God or unredeemed in
the lake of fire (REV. 20:15). Think soberly
of those words: No other place will
exist. Satan rages because he knows his
eternal destiny bears down on him like
an approaching freight train, and he is
out of options.

In my illustration, election day took
place on the cross. Christ has the only
valid claim as the ultimate ruler of all
creation. The one on the throne is God,
of course. He is the all-powerful, ultimate ruler of heaven and earth, and
nothing happens except by His perfect

or permissive will. Yes, Satan is "prince of this world," but only by divine permissive will and to accomplish God's own purposes. Satan was completely defeated by the offering of the perfect, sinless life of the Son of God on the cross. One day Christ will assume full reign of the world system where Satan has wreaked such havoc. Presently, however, the world exists in the period between the new election and the earthly inauguration of Christ.

Suppose we had a wicked president who knew he had already been defeated in the election and his removal from office was imminent. Can you imagine how he might wield and abuse his power in the little time he had left? On a mammoth, humanly incomprehensible scale, I believe that's what we're presently experiencing.

Satan reads the signs of the times like the *Washington Post*. He knows the inauguration of Christ's kingdom grows closer, so the arch demon furiously unleashes his power to the full extent of God's permissive will. The dragon is in a tailspin, and he is whipping everything he can in the time he has left. Because his ultimate fury is at God, nothing gives Satan greater unholy pleasure than assaulting God's children. Hence, our present conflict.

Our purpose through this booklet then is to understand how the people described in 2 Corinthians 11:2-3 as being wholeheartedly, sincerely, and purely devoted to Christ can be beguiled by Satan and have their minds corrupted and seduced. Certainly no one will argue that a believer can be characterized as godly while practicing ungodly things. Our task is to understand how a person who has consistently walked with God can be so powerfully seduced to ungodliness.

If I were forced to put the entire concept in a nutshell, I'd have to say that somewhere along the way, the godly person walked into a well-spun lie. Lies are Satan's stock in trade. He "fathers" every deception (JOHN 8:44) and seduction (2 COR. 11:2-3).

Satan's desire is to modify human behavior to accomplish his unholy purposes. Second Timothy 2:26 tells us that Satan's objective in taking people captive is to get them to do his will. If we have received Christ as our Savior, Satan is forced to work from the outside rather than the inside. Thus he manipulates outside influences to affect the inside decision-makers of the heart and mind.

Beloved, Satan will do everything he can to hang on once he gets a foothold in us. If the Devil has you in chains and you want out, know hope is here. God loves you, and He wants to restore you. If you are a believer who has never been had by the Devil, beware. Learn what he's up to, and be on guard. With Christ's help, you can overcome.

CHAPTER 2

ACKNOWLEDGE POINTS
OF VULNERABILITY

A few years ago my husband and I faced
the slow and steady destruction of our back
fence. It began when our neighbor innocently
planted a small line of trees at the back of
their property. Eventually, those trees grew to
a height of 12 feet. Inch by inch, their roots
crept under our fence posts and into our yard.
Branches that were once twigs developed into
sturdy arms that dislodged the fence's nails
and pushed the slats right off their horizontal
posts. The trees grew so gradually that we
didn't notice until our slats began falling, one
right after the other.

Our predicament could have been worse.
My husband pitched me a magazine the other
day and pointed to an article he insisted I
read. As I did, my eyes grew as big as saucers.
Another person's fence fell down too. What
complicated her situation is that her property

is next to a small wildlife park. Both neighbors had quite a lot of acreage, and she raised miniature horses while her neighbor boasted a variety of exotic animals.

How did she realize her fence was down? One day she looked up and a male lion was tearing her favorite horse to shreds for lunch. True story.

Tragically, we often don't realize the fence is down until Satan, the roaring lion, is devouring something precious to us right on our own property. Mind you, he has no right to be on our property, but all he needs for a written invitation is a weak spot in the fence.

What happened to our fence is exactly what happens in many of our lives when the enemy gains ground that does not belong to him. At some point prior to his complete intrusion in our lives, he laid groundwork. Like our neighbors' trees, this groundwork is often so subtle and seems so harmless that we give it very little notice. Inch by inch, the enemy grows something powerful right on the edge of our fence.

How do wholehearted and sincere servants of Christ become vulnerable to demonic seduction? After the personal stories I've encountered in the last several years, I am convinced that victims of seduction share certain vulnerabilities at their time of attack. None of us is sinless, but sin is not where the enemy most often gets his foothold among the godly. Rather, where Christian victims are concerned, the enemy more often latches on to personal weaknesses. While I can't assume all points of susceptibility are included in my list, I believe four specific weaknesses regularly open us to spiritual attack.

1. Ignorance

Without exception, the number one element that sets believers up for seduction is ignorance. What we do not know can hurt us!

In 2 Corinthians 2:11, Paul said he forgives offenses in part "to keep Satan from getting the advantage over us; for we are not ignorant of his wiles and intentions" (AMP). Don't miss the word *ignorant* here; I believe the state of ignorance is directly responsible for blinding us to what the Devil's up to.

The apostle Paul and his crew may not have been clueless about Satan's schemes, but most of us are. Beloved, we cannot afford such ignorance, particularly as the day is drawing near! (SEE HEB. 10:25.) We can't ignore Satan and assume he'll go away. Ignorance flies like a flag over our heads screaming, "Pick me! Pick me! I'm ripe for attack! Don't have any idea what's going on. I'm just the person to blindside with temptation." The apostle Paul repeated over and over, "I would not have you ignorant." We are wise to take his concern to heart, to set aside complacency, and to pick up the Word.

2. Spiritual passion that exceeds biblical knowledge
This one area of ignorance drains our spiritual strength faster than any other. Remember,

2 Corinthians 11:3 talks about the serpent getting into our hearts through our minds. That's why it's so important that we fill our minds with the things of God. The Lord wants us to love Him with our brains, not just our hearts. The church in Corinth was passionate but lacked the knowledge to provide a firm, less shakable foundation to help guard against the destructive influences of their community.

If we don't have the knowledge of God, we are ill equipped to recognize things that exalt themselves over God. We can't just have knowledge about warfare to defeat Satan. We desperately need the knowledge of God, and our only means of getting it is through an intense relationship with Him through His precious Word. God wants our zeal for Him to be based on scriptural truth. Without His truth in our heads and hearts, we are lame ducks awaiting the inevitable.

3. A lack of discernment

Discernment means to see or understand the difference. I am convinced that discernment is one of the most important criteria in providing the devoted believer with protection from seduction. Knowing the difference between what is and is not of God is critical to living in victory. If, after all, we cannot discern the Devil's lies from God's promises, we have little hope of tuning Satan out or tuning the Lord in. An intimate knowledge of God's Word is the best defense we have against a moment when the temptation to do wrong feels like the nudge to do right.

4. A lack of self-discernment

We commit some sins willfully and presumptuously. Others, inadvertently. The former flows from rebellion; the latter from error, ignorance, and weakness.

A close relationship exists between a lack of self-examination and going astray. Our weaknesses and areas of ignorance are huge vulnerabilities to seduction that can quickly lead to sins committed inadvertently. Satan's seduction is purposeful, well planned, and well timed; nothing about it is accidental or coincidental. Anytime we are loaded down with sins, whether intentional or not, we are game for seduction. We are vastly helped when we recognize, acknowledge, and ask forgiveness for our errors, both the intentional and the unplanned.

Beloved, Satan plays hardball. The psalmist testified about his foes and his powerful enemy with the words, "They confronted me in the day of my disaster" (Ps. 18:18). Somehow we secretly hope the Devil, as low as he is, surely has enough scruples to draw the line where the fight would be totally unfair, but Satan has no scruples! When we have a disaster, we can count on his being right there confronting us on our weakest, most vulnerable point.

The temptation to go astray is never far from any believer. In fact, even those who walk most closely with the Lord discover that the serpent often chooses to strike during those moments when God has never felt more near. We don't expect the serpent to slither around in our gardens as we share fellowship with God, but he's ever ready to do what he can to take our eyes off the Father. When we know where our personal weak places are, we become better equipped to survive the strike. God desires to cover our weaknesses with His strength. Our job is to acknowledge and ask for the help we need.

Never assume that a smaller problem won't explode into a bigger one just because it never has before. That's exactly what the enemy wants us to think. Don't ever forget what a schemer he is. He loves nothing better than supplying a false sense of security. One day, when we least expect it, we may look up and see the lion in the yard and our "pet" being torn to shreds.

CHAPTER 3

HEAR THE WARNINGS
OF THE SEDUCED

I explained in the introduction how my
concern over this topic grew out of reading
unnerving testimonials from people who
had consistently walked with God only to
be suddenly seduced by ungodly behavior.
When I recognized that I was looking at
the very essence of 2 Corinthians 11:2-3, I
poured over their stories with great attention and growing alarm, all the while
asking God for discernment. As I read their
stories and reflected on my own, I developed a case study from our experiences.

By no means do I suggest that all seductions share these commonalities. We have
no idea how many forms seduction can
take. I am shocked, however, by a number
of common claims that I believe are worth
our notice.

As we begin the list, please don't assume that all seduction is sexual in nature. Think far more widely as you try to grasp the breadth of Satan's expertise. Remember, he's simply after whatever works. Those who were enticed to do ungodly things after living godly lives shared many of the following 10 claims:

1. Individuals were caught off guard by a sudden onslaught of temptation or attack.

No one I spoke with planned his or her season of ungodliness. Virtually all felt as if they were hit so hard and fast that their heads spun. Many described having sinned before they even knew what hit them. Sound impossible? Actually, the possibility is stated unapologetically in Scripture. Galatians 6:1 says, "Brothers, if someone is caught in a sin, you who are spiritual should restore him gently. But watch yourself, or you may also be tempted." Concentrate on that word *caught*. One of the definitions of the Greek term *prolam-bano* describes the sin like this: "catches the individual by surprise ... before he is aware of what happened." We don't abandon sound theology to say that these kinds of sins can overtake individuals before they realize what is coming and put up their guard. That's why it's so important to stay in the Word, effectively keeping our shield close at hand.

2. The season of overwhelming temptation and seduction often followed huge spiritual markers with God.
These godly people who did ungodly things were not walking in sin when the seduction wave hit. In fact, I was amazed how many felt they had just entered a new season of growth in their relationships with God when the unimaginable happened.

Remember, Christ Himself endured a dreadful time of testing after receiving great blessing. After John baptized Him,

Jesus heard the glorious words from His Father in heaven: "This is my Son, whom I love; with him I am well pleased." The very next words? "Then Jesus was led by the Spirit into the desert to be tempted by the devil" (MATT. 3:17–4:1). Of course, Jesus endured His season of temptation without sin, but the experience was inconceivably brutal. I believe we mortals are particularly vulnerable at spiritually high times. We can't let feelings of spiritual coziness woo us into a false sense of security.

3. Everyone described a mental bombardment. Excessive thinking is a clear sign of a fierce demonic stronghold. The nature of a stronghold is something exalted in our minds contrary to the knowledge of God. We've got to "[cast] down imaginations, and every high thing that [exalts] itself against the knowledge of God, and [bring] into captivity every thought to the obedience of Christ" (2 COR. 10:4-5, KJV). Breaking free from mentally obsessive strongholds always requires bringing those previously exalted imaginations under Christ's authority. It's no small challenge, and it's one the enemy hopes we're not up to. We have to prove him wrong. We believers have divine power to demolish strongholds. Only in our own power is the task too much for us.

4. *Many of those caught in relational seductions (not all seductions are relational) testified that Satan got to them through someone close by.* When Satan is trying to wreak havoc on the godly, he isn't always successful with a blatantly ungodly approach. Remember, the nature of seduction implies an unexpected, well-disguised lure. The Devil looks for ways he can get close to the godly to gain trust.

Don't think that we simply can't trust people; just be warned that not everyone who appears trustworthy is. We must be desperate for discernment. Part of our fortification against seduction is making sure a door to our lives has not been opened through unhealthy relationships.

5. Many testified to early warning signals.
The Holy Spirit does not fail to do His job. Over and over I asked, "Did you get a flag of some kind that caused you to think you ought not proceed in that relationship or situation?" Almost invariably everyone said yes. It came while they were still walking faithfully with God. I asked why they didn't heed the warning, and virtually all admitted to having rationalized it away.

When our conscience starts nagging, we'd better pay attention. Likely the Holy Spirit is sending us warning.

6. Many described their sudden behavior patterns as totally uncharacteristic.
I can't tell you how often I heard statements like: "I kept thinking, *What in the*

world am I doing? I've never acted this way in my life!" Most mentioned that family, close friends, and associates also noticed uncharacteristic behavior. Anyone who confronted them, however, faced their defensiveness and rationalizations.

Mood swings, a determination to have our own way in spite of the effects our actions have, and a general sense of dissatisfaction with life are all glaring signs that something is not spiritually right in our lives. We should question changes in ourselves. They may mirror changes in our relationship with the Lord.

7. *Virtually all described feelings and practices of isolation.*

Satan loves isolation. He wants to draw the believer out of healthy relationships and healthy practices into secretive, unhealthy practices and associations. He purpose-fully woos us away from those who might openly recognize the seduction and call his hand on it. We are wise to be aware of anything that separates us from godly people and smart to see too much time alone as a negative thing.

8. Without exception, deception and some level of secrecy were involved.
Remember that the "secret power of lawlessness is already at work" (2 THESS. 2:7). Satan adores secrets and often works through disguises, masquerades, and shrouds. He wants things to stay in the dark because he knows the moment we expose them to the light of God, he's finished.

Deception is an absolute in every stronghold, but the nature of seductive deception is that the lies are often well masked for a while. We are undoubtedly caught in a seductive web when we start "having to lie" to explain our behavior. We reason with ourselves that others just wouldn't understand, but the real reason is that the deceived soon deceive.

9. Most utterly hated what they were doing.
Almost every person I interviewed testified that they hated their ungodly behavior
while at the same time being drawn to
it like a magnet. Part of Satan's ploy is to
make believers feel addicted and powerless.

Sometimes seduction so confuses the
mind and feelings that it draws off of the
pure animal-like instincts of the flesh.
The seduced person often deplores what
she's doing but in the heat of battle feels
overpowered by it. Sometimes people
can describe a time of rebellion with a
mischievous grin and even admit to having
enjoyed it for a season, but I have never
heard a godly person who was seduced
by the enemy say they could look back on
that time in their lives with a smile. All
will tell you it was their worst nightmare.
It filled their lives with shame, and they
ended up being sickened by it.

10. The seduction lasted only for a season.
Needless to say, the time frames vary, but people with genuine hearts for God cannot remain in a practice of sin. At some point they will cry out in total desperation for deliverance. For those who have walked closely with God, the desire for a return to intimate favor finally exceeds the lure of the seducer. In the end, Satan can't win because he can't sustain. Those who know God's truth will eventually see the Devil's lies.

First John 5:18 says, "We know that anyone born of God does not continue to sin; the one who was born of God keeps him safe, and the evil one cannot continue to harm him." Don't take this as a suggestion that godly people can't sin. None of us will ever be completely sinless until we reach the perfection of heaven. The King James Version interprets "can't continue to harm him" as "the wicked one toucheth him not." I'm not sure either word, *harm* or *touch*, adequately expresses the original. I'm letting Charles Ryrie explain this one in his fine work entitled *Basic Theology*: "It means not a superficial touching but a grasping, clinging to, or holding on to someone. Satan can never hang on to a believer with the purpose of harming him, for that believer belongs eternally and irrevocably to God. Satan (or demons) may afflict and even control for a time, but never permanently or eternally."

The Devil cannot possessively lay hold of us, keep us in a grip, or touch us in a way that will utterly destroy us. We may feel destroyed, but we are not. Christ preserves us from Satan's ultimate intent—our total annihilation.

Beloved, none of us is completely seduce-proof. We are able, however, to avoid and overcome temptation through the help God provides. Let the warnings of the seduced ring in your ears; don't detour from your walk with the Lord. "Be self-controlled and alert. Your enemy the devil prowls around like a roaring lion looking for someone to devour" (1 PET. 5:8). Don't allow yourself to become an easy target.

Chapter 4

KNOW THAT GOD IS IN CONTROL

Christ's call on Simon Peter's life was awesome; Jesus would make him a major player in the establishment and building up of His church. Christ even called Peter *Petros*, a chip off the old block. (Matt. 16:18). But before Peter had a chance to rest in the thrill of those words, Jesus blurted at him, "Get behind me, Satan! You are a stumbling block to me; you do not have in mind the things of God, but the things of men" (Matt. 16:23). Peter was a sincere follower of Jesus who left family and occupation to follow Christ, but his character needed a little work. He wasn't quite ready to accept that Christ would have to die to conquer evil, not squash it in a militant show of power.

Had Christ made a mistake in choosing Peter? Was He sorry? Hardly. He'd made no mistake. Christ knew exactly what He was doing. He also knew what each of His disciples was capable of doing. Only one reason exists why God would give Satan permission to sift a dearly loved, devoted disciple: because something needed sifting.

Christ called Peter knowing every flaw in him. He gave that flawed apostle a new assignment and a new name. By heaven, the call would be accomplished even if Christ had to do it Himself. I believe Jesus loved Peter's passion, but His cherished disciple also had some ingredients that could prove less palatable to the call. Everything standing between Simon the fisherman and Peter the rock needed to go.

Satan had a sieve. Christ had a purpose. The two collided. Satan got used. Peter got sifted. For reasons only our wise, trustworthy God knows, the most effective and long-lasting way he could get the Simon out of Peter was a sifting by Satan. He was right. You see, the One who called us is faithful, and He will do whatever it takes to sanctify us to fulfill our callings. Yes, it's that important. Huge things are going on out there that we just don't understand.

To me, we can easily and with sound theology compare the sifting of Peter to a full-scale attack by Satan on those with complete devotion to Christ. Christ loves all of us with everything in Him. You and I are called to be disciples of Christ in our own generations. He is just as protective and watchful of us as He was the original Twelve.

I believe God allows the Devil a certain amount of leash where we are concerned, but I am convinced that if he wants more than his daily allowance, he has to gain special permission. None of us is less important to Christ than Peter, James, John, or the apostle Paul. Jesus would never take lightly Satan's attack on one of His followers. For Satan to launch a full scale attack on a devoted follower of Christ, he has to get special permission.

So why does God allow someone with wholehearted devotion to Christ to get caught in the snare of demonic seduction? Because, not unlike Peter's case, something in our lives needs removing, sifting, or changing that an intense encounter with the kingdom of hell would best accomplish. I believe this with all my heart, first of all, because it is congruent with Scripture, and second, because I am convinced it happened to me.

In the book *Praying God's Word*, I shared about my sifting season with a little more detail, but I think a condensed version could be helpful right here. By almost anyone's standards, I have had some pretty difficult challenges in my life, but nothing has ever equaled the intensity and overwhelming sense of darkness that my sifting season had.

Years ago, the ladies in my weekday Bible study class began needling me about writing a Bible study. At that point I was only preparing weekly lectures, and I had never even considered such a thing. I turned them down on the spot, but they stayed after me until I finally succumbed to the pressure.

I went before God, sensed His blessing, and decided to give it a try. As I live and breathe, the thought of ever having anything published never occurred to me. I absolutely loved what I was already doing and was simply trying to offer this little slice of the body of Christ what they were asking. I look back on it now and marvel over my naiveté. I had all the passion of David dancing down the streets of Jerusalem—all the passion but no wall of protection around my temple. A big mouth for Jesus with virtually no armor is like a red flag waving at a demon-possessed bull.

In spite of me, God blessed our journey through the Word together, and Satan became infuriated. I think he was fairly certain he had taken care of me a long time ago. He was pretty sure someone with all my junk would never pose him much of a problem, but, you see, the Word of God unleashes a power even in the weakest.

We are wise to realize that Satan hates nothing more than the Word of God because it's the Sword of the Spirit. From the Evil One's perspective, only one thing appears worse than someone who equips him- or herself with the Word, someone who convinces others to equip themselves too. Of course, I was too green to realize the threat at the time.

In retrospect, I believe Satan asked for permission to get to me, and God held him off until I finished writing the study. Literally within 24 hours of putting a period on the last sentence, the enemy began a scheme to destroy me that stands unparalleled in my life. In a nutshell, for a series of months my mind was bombarded with horrible pictures stemming from my childhood. A flood of memories came back to me. Satan proceeded to seduce me into believing horrible lies about myself and virtually everyone I knew. I became physically ill, suffered recurring nightmares, and sank into depression. Defeat haunted me.

There I was serving God with every ounce of energy I had. Trying to be a godly wife. Trying to raise my children to love the Lord. Why did God let such a mean thing happen to me? Oh, Beloved, because this little woman had something that needed sifting.

Allow me to draw back to my fellow Bible study writers, Henry Blackaby and T. W. Hunt. All three of us will go through various tests because we each need refining. None of us is truly refined until we're conformed into the image of Christ. While all three of us need refining, all three of us haven't necessarily needed sifting. The apostle John didn't appear to need such severe sifting. But Peter did. And so did I.

Beloved, are you being sifted? Has God permitted the enemy to launch a full scale attack against you? God knows what He's doing. He isn't looking the other way or being mean. Maybe this is the only way He can get you to attend to the old so He can do something new. Grab onto Him for dear life! Give Him full reign to remove in you anything that needs to go.

And, finally, remember that the Lord is always in charge. You will never face a storm in which He is not willing to help you. Be encouraged and sift, Beloved, sift!

CHAPTER 5

LEARN THE STEPS TO RECONCILIATION

Knowing how to return to the safety and forgiveness of God's embrace is one of the most important lessons we can learn in our discussion of how to arm ourselves against the enemy's schemes. None of us is immune to the pull of temptation, yet all of us are able to overcome it—even when it first seems to overcome us—if we will submit to an intense period of detoxification, deprogramming, and reprogramming.

When we fall for one of Satan's ploys and find ourselves up to our hairlines in a mess of our own making, we've allowed the same serpent who got his fangs into Eve to take a bite out of us. The resulting injection is like a poison, venom, or toxin. In order to detoxify, we've got to cut ourselves off from all connections to the source. Sometimes this requires stiff accountability, but it's vital that we take this seriously.

The following steps can help us accomplish detoxification:

1. Get Humble; Ask for Forgiveness

No one trapped in sin will ever reestablish a close walk with God without first asking forgiveness. Remember, Christ is always anxious that we find our way back to Him. When Jesus sacrificed His life at the cross, our sins were forgiven once and for all, but we are not free to live in the flesh. When we take our spiritual failures lightly, we forget the heavy price Christ paid so we could live in freedom. Only when we once again admit our failures and humbly ask Him to forgive us do we reaffirm our commitment to letting Him be Lord over our lives.

We can make no excuses. We should rationalize nothing. Beloved, the way home begins with humility.

2. Feel Sorrow Over Sin

Our sorrow leading to repentance is the way the Holy Spirit bears witness that we belong to God. The idea of feeling such sorrow over sin that we drop to our knees in grief may seem foreign, but such release comes in adopting this practice! You see, when a believer allows a sin or seduction to fog his relationship with the Father, he allows a divide that separates him from the source of all love, hope, and joy. God offers us the freedom to know He loves us, the hope of heaven, and the joy of having Him on our side. Just the thought of losing any of these gifts should make us want to weep!

When we humbly ask for forgiveness and allow the gravity of what we've done to soften our battered hearts, we take a giant step closer to the Father's protective, healing side.

3. Trust God, Not the Feelings

When we've asked pardon and come to grips with what we've done, we need to lean heavily on what Scripture has to say about our circumstances and relationships. Often hearts seduced become so misshapen by Satan's lies that the feelings they project over a situation cannot be trusted. Satan knows that the nature of humankind is to act out of how we feel rather than what we know. One of our most important defenses against satanic influence is learning how to behave out of what we know is truth rather than what we feel.

We must remember that even when believers fail, our hearts are still the homes of Christ. He's still in there, still telling us what to do. The catch is that we've got to make sure we are listening to Him instead of to our injured emotions.

We must not allow the destroyer to injure anymore. We can't give him another inch. The first piece of armor a seduced believer must put on is the breastplate of righteousness. An injured heart is protected by *doing* what's right until we *feel* what is right. The best litmus test we have for truth is God's Word. When we go by what it says, we can't go wrong.

4. Rest in God's Mercy

The final step to detoxification is to rest in God's mercy. Even when we feel we've fallen so far from God's grace that we can never return home, we must recognize the feeling as a lie. If the Bible is about anything at all, it is about God having mercy on the pitiful human plight, forgiving their sins and restoring their lives. Christ never resisted the truly repentant. He forgave them with outstretched arms.

Satan loves to nitpick one seduced as she or he seeks the Father's forgiveness. One of the enemy's favorite tactics is to whisper, "God may forgive you, but He still remembers what you did. How could He forget?" Remember, Scripture says that God forgives and forgets (JER. 31:34; HEB. 8:12). Only mortals remember sins committed and confessed under Christ's blood. We recall what has been so as never to lose sight of where we've been and how God rescued us.

However Satan may accomplish it, he is often successful in programming believers' minds with lies and a lot of junk that needs dumping. Every satanic stronghold involves believing a lie or lies. Seduction involves believing a subtle arsenal of them.

I believe it's not enough to detoxify after a seductive attack. We must also deprogram ourselves. I am going to risk being labeled a fanatic on this one, but I have seen the process work, and I have seen the process fail. The participant's willingness to cooperate with this objective makes a huge difference.

One seduced should consider deprogramming from all sorts of deceptive media. Contact with any messages, whether in movies, on television, in magazines or books, or even the poor advice of well-meaning friends, should be put on hold until a believer is fully restored. All sorts of messages that don't fuel temptation or compromise godly character are available to Christians. We should carefully consider what goes into our minds. Deprogramming ourselves of what the world says in favor of better tuning into what God has to say is always a wise move.

Beloved, believers who have overcome as well as those who are currently in

crises must set on a course of reprogramming. Only God's Word can equip
us with the truth we need to overcome
every lie the enemy tells.

CONCLUSION

GOD'S WAY HOME

If you've come to this booklet feeling the shame of a personal seduction, you aren't alone. I've been there too. It hurts. It's difficult. Sometimes you'll feel as if you can't breathe. But God offers hope, Dear One; He offers hope!

If you've just walked through a valley of spiritual defeat or even feel as if you're currently headed down one, you need godly teaching as badly as you have ever needed it in your life. You are in desperate need of good, solid, godly (not just "Christian" or "spiritual") counsel. You need to know how to proceed from where you are now to where God wants you to go. Just like mine and countless others, your own vision, perception, and estimation have failed you. You need the help of wise others so you can improve your sight and awareness.

Beloved, you cannot get through the restoration process wholly on your own. You need members of the body of Christ. Our brothers and sisters in the Lord are partially responsible for our restoration to Him. Their job is to fervently lift us up in prayer that we might find healing, freedom, strength, and the determination to develop hearts and minds dedicated to living under the guard of God's Word.

You, like all the others of us who have fallen for the enemy's schemes, need to get biblically educated and take a good look like never before at where and why you went wrong. I believe the best place to start is with developing a healthy fear, or respect, of the Lord. First Samuel 12:24 says, "Be sure to fear the Lord and serve him faithfully."

God is huge. He is awesome; indeed, He is terrifying. He is powerful. He holds all the keys to life and death, ecstasy and agony. Our futures are entirely in His hands. He is sovereign, and He answers to no one. He holds the oceans in the palm of His hands. The lightning checks in with Him. But for His mercy, we would all be consumed. He is holy and does not wink at wickedness. He lifts up and He casts down. When He rises from His throne, His enemies scatter. He has no equal. He is complete, pure, and unadulterated. When we wrap our hearts around how incredible God is, we wrap our hearts in a blanket of protection. When we fear the Lord, we learn to trust the Lord.

Remember, in the Old Testament God extended complete grace and mercy to the wayward Israelites and gave them the perfect remedy for their restoration. However, He tagged a vital warning to the end: Don't persist in doing evil. If they did, God promised they would be "swept away" (1 SAM. 12:25).

I have no idea how being swept away could apply to us, and I don't ever want to find out. It didn't mean, either to the Israelites or to us, being swept away from God's parenting. The Lord has already promised that He entered into a blood covenant with us through Jesus Christ, and He will never leave us or forsake us. Being swept away could, however, apply in many other painful ways to our earthly experience. It could mean swept away from usefulness, from the fellowship of the body of Christ, from His fellowship (which would be a fate I consider worse than earthly death), from our giftedness, from our places of service, or even from our earthly lives (SEE ACTS 5).

The great news is that complete forgiveness and restoration is ours—even usefulness in the body of Christ and lives of faithful service! God can work everything together for good and redeem our failures. He will gladly be strong in our weaknesses and show us His gracious favor. He can plunder the enemy and take back what Satan stole from us. But we cannot persist in doing evil. Just as an antibiotic will not have its full effectiveness if not taken under the prescribed conditions, God's prescription carries a warning label:

"Ineffective when patient persists in doing evil."

God does not ask us for perfection. I'm certainly no rule of thumb, but I live a rare day without something to confess, whether the sin has been outward in word or deed or inward in attitude, motive, or omission. Remember, God did not say to the Israelites nor does He say to us, "If you don't pull your act together and start acting perfectly, you'll be swept away." He said that if they persisted in the evil that got them into their mess, they would face serious consequences. The same is undoubtedly true for us. To the woman caught in adultery, Christ said, "Neither do I condemn you. ... Go now and leave your life of sin" (JOHN 8:11).

God will empower you to obey Him by the Holy Spirit within you. Cast yourself on Him if you don't believe you can leave a life of sin. Ask Him to raise up an army to help you and defend you against the enemy. Ask Him to do whatever He must do! You cannot persist in evil without dire consequences.

Beloved, your feelings of hopelessness and helplessness come straight from the enemy. They are lies. Surrender yourself to God, withholding nothing, and ask Him to do what seems impossible. Humble yourself and receive the help He will send as you seek it.

He who called you is faithful, and He will do it! (SEE 1 THESS. 5:24.)

SATISFY YOUR TASTE FOR MORE.
EXPERIENCE THE FULL STUDY.

Beth contends that many who have "fallen" are authentic servants who were unaware of the devil's schemes. She compassionately points the way back to God and reveals a Savior who forgives, cleanses, adorns, and restores. The full 7-week study of *When Godly People Do Ungodly Things* contains Beth Moore's compelling video messages, and in-depth personal study in the Member Book.

Now that you've gotten a taste of this redemptive message, experience the full study.

To order, and find out more:
www.lifeway.com/women
1.800.458.2772
LifeWay Christian Stores

LifeWay | Women

About the Author

Beth Moore has written best-selling Bible studies on the tabernacle, Psalms of Ascent, David, Paul, and Jesus. Her books *Breaking Free, Praying God's Word,* and *When Godly People Do Ungodly Things* have all focused on the battle Satan is waging against Christians. *Believing God* and *Living Beyond Yourself* focus on how Christians can live triumphantly in today's world. Beth has a passion for Christ, a passion for Bible study, and a passion to see Christians living the lives Christ intended.

Beth is an active member of First Baptist Church of Houston, Texas. The wife of Keith, mother of two young adult daughters Amanda and Melissa, and grandmother to Jackson, Beth serves a worldwide audience through Living Proof Ministry. Her conference ministry, writing, and videos reach millions of people every year.